THE VALLEY TO THE MOUNTAIN

The Valley to the Mountain

Blessings and Lessons

Lynette Shelto-Johnson

Copyright @ Lynette Shelto-Johnson 2023

English translation 2022

Lynette Shelto-Johnson has asserted her right under the Copyright designs to be identified as the Author of this book.

This book is entirely a work of non-fiction. The names, characters and places in this book are true stories of the Author.

This book is sold subject to the condition that it shall not by way of trade or otherwise be lent, resold, hired out or otherwise circulated without the publisher's prior consent in any form of binding or cover other than that which it is published and without similar condition, including this condition being imposed on the subsequent purchaser.

ISBNs

978-1-80541-112-3 - paperback
978-1-80541-111-6 - eBook

Contents

Introduction 1
Childhood 5
   The Happy Days 5
   That One Fateful Day 8
A New Start 11
   Migrating to Matthew's Ridge, Northwest Region .. 11
   Sunshine After the Storm 12
Tragedies Over Waters 15
   Malfunctioned Plane Number One 15
   Lost at Sea 17
School Days 21
   Mahaica Bygeval Multilateral School, Guyana 21
   Jim Jones 1978 Tragedy 22
A New Life in Georgetown City 25
   A Glimpse at Nursing 26
My Military Experience 29
Married at Twenty 31

Nursing and Silver Linings 35
    My LPN Experience 35
    My Midwifery Experience....................................36
Dream of a New Life Abroad 41
    Saint Lucia Bound 42
Faith in God Beyond Extreme.....................................45
    Miracle Baby 45
Back to Where Dreams Were Birthed 49
    Bittersweet...51
An American Getaway 57
New Pastures..59
Life in the UK 61
    En Route to London... 64
My Daughter's Academic Years 67
A Serial Acting Manager 69
A Different Path 75
Deserved Breaks and the Fruits of My Labour 79
    Paris 2018..79
    Reunions Galore 80
    Alabama 2019 82
    Scotland 2019.. 85
    Birthday Celebration November 2019.................. 86
Swift Changes 87
    COVID-19 Pandemic 87
Post-Pandemic Freedom 89

CONTENTS

A New Era 91
Thanks 93
Reasons for Writing This Book 101
Summary 103

Introduction

We all had dreams before we could comprehend what dreams were. Dreams aren't meant to be easily achieved, for that would simply be reality. Dreams are almost fantastical, and that is what makes them that much more satisfying when you see them materialise in front of you. Without what some may call a crazy imagination or faith, dreams can appear borderline nuts. That's why to achieve your dreams, you need resilience, trust in yourself and an undeniable belief that God will add his magical touch to what you have done.

My name is Lynette Shelto-Johnson. I am writing this book from London, England. I am a long-time registered nurse turned care home manager. I am a mother and a land/house owner amongst other things. These were all dreams I had as a child and as a young woman. The chances of achieving these things were slim to none; yet, by the grace of God, my dreams are now reality.

I am aiming to encourage and motivate anyone who reads this book by sharing some of my life's stories. After sixty years on this earth, I have managed to accumulate life experiences of all sorts. These will have you laughing, shocked, in awe, humbled and a lot more. As I sat down to plan this book, I marvelled at how far I had come: the moments that had shaped me into who I am today and the everyday miracles that I didn't acknowledge. In the words of my daughter, "Wow, life is crazy." And indeed, it is.

But first, let me introduce myself before I let you into my life.

I was born in Guyana, South America, in Georgetown Hospital on 3rd November 1961. I come from a large family of modest means. My mother gave birth to thirteen children, of which I am the fourth oldest. Sadly, three of my siblings died at birth, another from infant illness and my beloved sister, Lorraine, died tragically at age six after being poisoned.

My family and I lived in a small rural area, on the east coast of Guyana, called Victoria village. The area is dotted with grass, lakes and wooden and concrete houses of all different primary colours. Victoria was the first village in Guyana to be bought by the combined resources of Africans who had recently won their freedom from slavery.

INTRODUCTION

As for my mother, she was a hard-working woman. She was very blunt and funny. Her name was Alice Yvonne Francis-Shelto. You would often hear neighbours and old-time friends around the way asking about her, for she was loved by many. They found her generous and nurturing. My mother would make pastries and cakes, then walk to the market early in the morning and sit in the biting sun selling her delicious bits in order to make some extra money. My father was a wise and spiritual man with great business acumen. Vernon Gillis Shelto was his name, and he was highly respected.

My mother passed away from cancer on 12th March 2012 at seventy-three years old. I watched as the woman who birthed me took her last breath on earth, but her first step into something greater than we could ever imagine. My father died at eighty-nine from pneumonia on 28th December 2009. Whilst they are no longer physical beings roaming this earth, and whilst I miss them, I take solace in remembering that this life is only the beginning. Even after their death, my parents' honourable traits lingered on in my siblings and I. I will forever be grateful to my parents for all they have taught and shown to us.

With my parents' influence and God's amazing mercies, I move through life chasing every dream I can dare to conjure up. I hope my stories will produce a similar drive in you.

Childhood

The Happy Days

I look back on the sixties and the seventies with immense nostalgia. The world has changed so much since, I can't help but feel a sense of distance to the person I was then and the memories that formed my primitive years. Yet, the emotions stayed with me, even now as I sit here some fifty or so years later. We didn't have much materially, but in joy and spirit, we had plenty.

As of this moment, I can stroll to my bathroom sink and have a stream of water ready in both hot and cold temperatures. But back then, my siblings and I would have to walk to the community's rod standpipes a little distance away from home to collect buckets of water. To a mind that has never encountered luxury, these simple adventures seemed like a world of fun. Every morning, the village could be found lined up chatting loudly whilst waiting to collect their buckets and basins of water.

As kids, we used this time to catch up with neighbouring friends and play a few games. Of course, water wars and hopscotch with friends were games one could not miss. When our parents asked why we came home drenched, we would mumble something about the buckets of water spilling on our heads. They knew we were lying, for they too probably came home soaked during their childhood. In any case, all that really mattered was that water was brought back for bathing and cooking.

Yes, the days were good. The streets were free of traffic, and pollution did not blur the stars. The back doors of houses could be left sprawled open, even in everyone's absence, and items would remain where they were. Parents would allow their children to roam the streets without fear they may never return. All in all, I guess you could say we built a community and a family with those around us. In Victoria village lived the Assanah family, alongside the Bobbs, the Rogers, the Eastmans, the Charles, the Francis and the David's family. Many of whom, I am still in contact with to this day.

In the middle of all of this, my parents ensured God was front and centre. We were sent to a Roman Catholic school in Victoria. Worship service painted our mornings before class. "This is the day; this is the day which the Lord hath made!" would echo through classrooms and onto the roads. This was my favourite part of the school day, only to be topped by our visit to the Catholic church for communion. Jesus' body was represented in the form of a wafer with icing and his blood tasted like grape juice. We never questioned this, we simply enjoyed.

Returning home to my mother's cooking was even better. Electric and gas stoves were for those affluent families, so we, instead, had a kerosene stove. It was a small green metal hob that took a while to cook the food. So, instead, my mother made an oven out of mud; she said it baked her cakes and bread quicker and was convinced it tasted better anyway. My mother was a housewife in those days, and a pretty good one at that. My father was a man of many trades, but you could find him in the day time driving the General Post Office truck dropping off deliveries to different locations and doing taxi work on his days off to make ends meet.

That One Fateful Day

But similar to many, there are those experiences and moments that can taint your memories forever. For myself and my siblings, there was this one fateful day we can recall vividly. I was only eight years old when my family and I were poisoned by someone we would have never expected. This person was warm, jovial and friendly. It made the headlines that week and was the talk and hot gossip of our little village, but for those of us who were hanging on between life and death, it was a horror tale.

My father had left for work that morning, none the wiser to the fact a person who did not hold him in high regard was about to poison the family pot. It is tradition that the paternal figure of the home gets the first scoop of food. And so, the perpetrator's logic was that if she poured the poison at the very top of the pot, my father would receive the deathly portion. That was her explanation at least. Well, it just so happens that my father had gone to work before having his meal that day, which left the rest of us at the mercy of the poison. And like one expects of gravity, the liquid death seeped its way throughout the entire pot. She had intended to kill my father, who turned out to be the only one who didn't fall victim.

CHILDHOOD

My seven-month pregnant mother became very sick. Every one of us was rushed to the hospital. My mother was in a bad state and was immediately hooked up to bags and bags of saline. Personally, I don't remember feeling unwell, not in the way you would expect poison to affect a fragile child. My younger six-year-old sister, Lorraine, also showed no signs of sickness. In fact, we were energised, stomping around the ward like adventurers in a playground. Someone told me years later that the dying body exerts the most energy in its last moments in an attempt to defeat death. I guess this energy is why the nurses didn't pay much attention to us, and why eventually Lorraine, supposedly well, passed away in the cradle next to me. We were overlooked.

I remember them wrapping her lifeless body in a white sheet and me shouting at them, "Stop wrapping my sister with a sheet! She can't breathe with the sheet around her face! And don't take her away! She can't breathe with the sheet over her face!"

I believe it was somewhere during this traumatic moment that I decided nursing was my calling. I wanted to take care of sick people. I wanted to treat everyone, even those who didn't look like they needed it physically. I wanted to be the one to save a six-year-old child from a death not written for her and she did not deserve.

Five years after the poisoning saga, a neighbour who lived very near to us in Victoria would ask my mother for forgiveness. She had entered our home from downstairs where my mother's fresh food rested open and unattended on our stove and saw her opportunity. She begged my mother to not call the police, but more than anything she had begged for forgiveness. You see, this neighbour was dying and desperately needed the gift of forgiveness before departing. My mother, being a beautiful lady with a heart full of love, not only promised not to call the police but also extended her genuine forgiveness for poisoning her, the entire family and killing her daughter. My mother also urged the rest of us to forgive. This was our way of healing and letting go of the bitterness and grief that built after Lorraine's death.

After all, to err is human and to forgive is divine.

A New Start

Migrating to Matthew's Ridge, Northwest Region

Forgiveness is a choice, but sometimes erasing trauma is not. Especially when you remain in the environment where such traumatic events befell you. Victoria village soon represented a place of death and grieving for us. That was why the former president of Guyana, President Burnham, helped my family and I migrate to the northwest region of Guyana, a place called Matthew's Ridge. His intentions were that a fresh environment would help us heal emotionally from my sister's untimely death.

My parents were given free plane tickets for the entire family from Victoria to Matthew's Ridge. Dad was given a job and a free house which was ours for the taking. Could all of these material things replace Lorraine's life and our memory of her? Of course not. But this relocation was definitely God's way of helping us out of a financially and emotionally draining situation and placing us somewhere that would eventually become sweet, sweet home.

Sunshine After the Storm

With the favour of time, Matthew's Ridge became our little sanctuary. Looking back now, I would call it my home in Guyana, for I practically grew up there and it housed the better half of my childhood. I called this place "the little fairy town". It was a beautiful green village. We lived in a small concrete house on a hill. Myself, my parents, my three brothers, Adolphus, Cecil and Trenton, and my four sisters, Doris, Jennifer, Annie and Nicola, were all squeezed into a two-bedroom square box.

Nevertheless, we had really set up camp there. We immersed effortlessly into the community, the schools and the vibrancy. Dad opened a little beer garden that would bring together joyous neighbours during the evenings. They played the good oldies and chattered well into the warm nights. My mother was still doing her baking, but this time selling it out of my father's beer shop. She made cakes and different types of finger food. Their specialty was Guyanese Salara cake, which is a red coconut pastry roll. One word to describe this delicacy? Magnifique!

On the side, my mother also sewed by hand, before she bought a sewing machine, and she made clothes for everyone. She never had any professional training, but her needlework said otherwise, and it was from her that I also learnt how to sew my own clothes. My sister Jenny would become the seamstress though and made bespoke outfits for family and friends.

The new environment also allowed us all to dive into our athletic and entrepreneurial spirit. Doris became a champion athlete in school for two years straight. Cecil dominated the long-distance race and was talented at the high jump. As for myself, when I wasn't partaking in a sporting event, I would walk around trying to sell some of my mother's food. When the teacher's attention was elsewhere, I would go around bargaining with other children until all my products were gone.

Yes, Matthew's Ridge was home indeed.

Tragedies Over Waters

Malfunctioned Plane Number One

A few years later, when we had settled into our new life, my sister Doris and I decided to fly to the capital city, Georgetown, to stay for a while. For much of the flight, the plane glided through the sky and everything was normal. That was until we were above Georgetown Airport and the pilot realised the wheels of the plane weren't coming out.

Now, the last thing anyone wants to hear a thousand miles into the air is that the plane they are sitting in has malfunctioned. It is a terrifying moment made worse by the thought you are truly helpless. It is moments like this when you realise how absolutely and unfortunately powerless and feeble the human really is. The plane was small so we could overhear the engineers on the ground directing the pilot on how and when to land. Their words were not comforting, rather it intensified the idea of impending death.

"You will have to fly the plane until the fuel has finished and then you will need to crash land at the airport."

There was a subdued panic radiating throughout the plane as everyone realised what this could mean. We were all very tense and uneasy. There were mumbles of distress and people started offering up prayers and bargains to the only one who could help us now: "Oh God. Oh God."

The plane flew around the airport once, twice, thrice trying to eject the wheels. Around the tenth time we circled the airport to no avail, the captain announced we would soon run out of fuel and we all had to prepare for a crash landing. I looked out of the window and below us were over ten miniscule fire trucks waiting for our tragic touchdown. I looked at my sister Doris who also noticed the fire trucks below.

"Let's pray," she said.

Doris and I started to pray, but above all we trusted God would help us down to a safe landing – wheels or not. We prayed and prayed, and then repeated our prayers. On our twelfth circle around the airport, we heard a booming screech as the wheels finally forced their way out of their compartment.

Praise the Lord. Glory to God in the highest!

There was a release of tension in the air and breaths of relief from everyone when the plane landed safely. There was nothing more beautiful in that moment than feeling the land below my feet. The firemen came over to us, a little relieved themselves that they didn't have to do the job they came for.

"Praise God! We were waiting to put out the fire if the plane crash landed!" one of them laughed. He did not mention the possible lifeless bodies he may have found had that been the case.

But yes, praise the Lord.

Lost at Sea

But if being trapped in the air above an airport wasn't enough, my family and I would later get lost at sea. I argue that this was a worse fear. At least on the plane, we knew where we levitated above, and we had professionals ready to aid us if the need arose. But being on open water, with no idea what direction you're floating towards or what lingers beneath the boat, sends a dooming feeling through to your soul.

Here is the story of when I got lost at sea.

Now there are things you never envision could happen to you. These are the things you see in movies. The things that have you holding your breath and silently shouting encouragement to the actors through the screens. But the truth is, it can be you and sometimes it will be you. And for me, one of these moments was our trip from our little village in Matthew's Ridge. It started off as an exciting adventure, just a small-town family heading to the hustling bustling big city.

However, buying plane tickets for the entire family was out of the question. As a family of very little means, the luxury of flying through the sky was not one we could afford often. We settled instead for a voyage across the sea. The usual big boats were broken down, so we had to use the smaller ones.

We boarded onto a steamboat with three other families, expecting a smooth sail. But halfway through our journey, the steamboat got lost, leaving us stranded on a brown sea with no sign of land for miles. Frightened and lost, we crowded together like sardines in a tin. Without life jackets, God was the only source of protection out in the middle of nowhere. We were somewhere between the shores of Guyana and the land of Venezuela. We searched for signs of civilisation as the boats floated pointlessly on.

Thankfully, a man had a radio with him, and so he extended its antenna and pointed it into different directions, desperately searching for a signal from Georgetown's radio station. This went on for seven to eight hours before we were able to get a clear signal. With the familiar and comforting Guyanese accent of one of the radio hosts, we were able to steer home, safe and in one piece.

School Days

Mahaica Bygeval Multilateral School, Guyana

My sister and I enrolled in Bygeval Secondary School for one year, a truly amazing school that moulded us into the adults we would one day become.

Well, except that one teacher who taught our Spanish class. From what I can remember, he was arrogant and lacked the warmth one would expect of a secondary school teacher. His attitude kept his class away. We waited outside our toilets, dancing and playing games instead. The times we would summon the courage to go to lessons, we would show up late, a little bit distressed and very impatiently waiting for the hour to finish. It was only when another Spanish teacher replaced him that I saw that class full for the first time. I then understood the importance of a kind heart when seeking to influence and teach others. No one wants to learn from a cold person who has so much to learn themselves.

But I digress, and despite these hiccups, we were determined to make the most of our new school and so we grasped at every chance offered to us. We joined the dance crew at school and that took us on trips to other competing schools out of the village and then to the prestigious National Culture Centre that showcased various creative performances and more. I later transferred and attended Port Kaituma Secondary School.

Jim Jones 1978 Tragedy

Port Kaituma School is located in, well, Port Kaituma. I spent one year there. It is a little town, not too far from Matthew's Ridge, and even closer to the Jonestown Temple. The Jonestown Temple was situated about six miles from Port Kaituma. The Jonestown entrance was only situated three miles from Port Kaituma.

Too close for comfort, if you ask me.

One unsuspecting day, the sound of guns permeated the air. No one knew what they were hearing would become part of the plot of the crime of the century: the Jim Jones Peoples Temple tragedy. Our school was immediately told to shut down for safety. Teachers and children were to be transported via train to anywhere but there.

We were sent back to Matthew's Ridge. The train was packed airtight, filled with desperate fearful children.

As the train hurtled through Jonestown, we watched through the windows trying to discover the area the guns had fired off. We prayed the train would travel faster through the death-filled atmosphere. When the train escaped Jonestown, everyone in the train released trapped breaths and sighed with relief. We had gotten out unharmed. But back in Jonestown, over 900 people lay lifeless, poison seeping through their blood. A truly merciless and demonic crime had taken place just minutes away from my classroom. A mass murder that would be remembered across the globe for decades. It was a day I will never forget. A spiritual war zone.

The day that followed was undeniably upsetting. Everyone knew the American army helicopters that went to and fro across the sky were carrying the dead back to America. The image still pops up in my mind sometimes of army helicopters fetching corpses through a beautiful blue Caribbean sky.

Two months before the murders, a group of people from the Jim Jones Temple had visited Port Kaituma School to hold a concert. It was entertaining. There was laughter, happiness and liveliness. Some of them were amazing singers and dancers. Two months later, just like that, they were all gone. It affected me emotionally a great deal; I never returned to Port Kaituma School. Not many parents sent their children back either. It was a traumatising time for many.

A New Life in Georgetown City

I migrated from Matthew's Ridge to Georgetown City in January 1979, following the Jim Jones tragedy in November 1978.

As it was now January, it was difficult to get into a school so far into the school term, so I decided to attend evening classes to study for my GCSEs. My eldest brother Adolphus was working as a police officer during that time. He used to play cricket for the police force, and he was one of the fastest bowlers for cricket in the team. He took most of his salary that month and paid for my exams.

"How can you give me all your money? How will you make do this month?" I had asked him.

"God will provide," he had responded and indeed God did provide that month.

I am so grateful to him and grateful to God for blessing him with the money, so he could help me. Like I said, my mother taught us that love is of God because God is love. And with that, I was able to complete my exams.

After completing and passing my exams, I became more eager to pursue my childhood dream of becoming a nurse, but soon realised that getting into the industry, like many things in life, was not cheap. But faith can move mountains and so I kept the dream alive.

A Glimpse at Nursing

One day, I was walking down the street in Georgetown and an elderly gentleman approached me. He said he was working at the Ministry of Health and they were looking to recruit people who would like to do nursing.

The first thing that came to my mind was that he was an angel or something of the sort. How could he have known that I wanted to be a nurse? I had never met this man in my life.

He asked if I knew anyone who would be interested and if I did, I should ask them to go to the Ministry of Health. Then he smiled at me briefly as I glared at him in silence. I was a bit sceptical but was still curious to know what the requirements were to enter nursing school. He said five subjects at GCSE level and four months in the

Guyana National Service would be needed before anyone could be accepted. I then asked him if he had any proof that he was working at the Ministry of Health because everything seemed too coincidental to be real. He simply showed me his badge; it looked authentic enough. The only thing was my parents could not afford to pay for me to complete five subjects at GCSE privately. They could only afford three subjects and so that was all I did and I told him so.

He smiled again and kindly explained I could get into the practical nursing programme with three subjects at first and then slowly develop my career in the future. It would be a much longer process, but it would be worth it.

He took some more time to discuss the entire process with me. I would have to pass an aptitude test, then train with the Guyana National Service for four months before starting the practical nursing programme. Just like that, I was convinced. I completed the aptitude test and completed five months in the Guyana National Service along with forty other nurses.

My Military Experience

The military course lasted five months instead of four months because the military plane which was transporting food crashed, causing the course to delay. Luckily, the military base was only seven miles away from Matthew's Ridge where I grew up. My family was still living there and some of my family is still living there today. I was able to visit my family and eat at home since food was then scarce at the military base due to the food cargo plane crashing. I would not change this moment in time for anything.

My time in the military was a test of resilience, for sure. We had jungle training twice a week with loading machine guns and had to take part in "mock wars". This was difficult and possibly extremely dangerous now that I think about it, but it taught us survival. Running six miles every morning with the rifles before going onto the drill square was another hectic task but this taught us determination and perseverance. Not to mention that running with a rifle for six miles is painfully difficult, but it taught me self-discipline and pushed me to reach my goals.

I was then selected as part of a group to go on the Guard of Honour parade. It was a fantastic experience. All I could think about during that parade was "I hope no one drops their rifle" and luckily no one did!

Leaving the military base was sad (though admittedly slightly relieved from no longer having to run with rifles for miles on end!), but I knew I had a dream to accomplish.

Returning to the city around May 1981, the wait for the initial nursing programme to begin took a while. When the preliminary course was completed, I did not look for a job as I was waiting and had faith I would be called to start the practical nursing programme soon. During this wait, I could not return to Matthew's Ridge where the majority of my family were as the flight would be expensive to go and return to start the nursing programme. I needed a place to stay and because I was not working, I was unable to rent a place on my own, especially in the city. One of my dear friends Juliet Graham-Thornhill took me in and gave me free housing and food.

Married at Twenty

I got married to a man seven months before starting my nursing programme. He would constantly try to convince me I did not need to work and that he would take care of me. But I was a determined woman and I had set my mind on becoming a nurse, so needless to say, his request was never going to be granted. I had to be a nurse and a very good one at that. After all, I had made that promise to myself when Lorraine died from food poisoning next to me in that cradle all those years ago.

But above all, he was verbally and physically aggressive and I guess I knew early on that no such man could take care of me or make me happy. I knew I was not going to encourage this behaviour for long.

The nail in the coffin was when I returned to the city a few weeks later to discover another girl was six months pregnant and carrying my husband's child. I filed for divorce immediately. I was divorced before I turned twenty-one years old. I moved out and went to live with my father who was working in the city at the time. As it turned out, my ex-husband was seeing this girl during the time we were planning our wedding. The girl and her mother would later tell me he told them I was his sister.

My ex-husband did not easily acquiesce to our separation. He was in the police force when I met him and therefore had access to weapons that a man of his temper should not have had access to. After my father graciously took me in, my ex-husband found my whereabouts. He showed up at my father's house with a work gun. He aimed the gun at my head and promised that if I did not comply with his instructions, he would have no choice but to use the firearm. He forced me back to his home. Thankfully, the neighbours had witnessed this all happening. They informed my father who immediately reported the incident to the police. The police were swift in their rescue mission and I was saved from the harrowing hold of my ex-husband.

As for the girl I discovered was pregnant, she married him soon after. This series of unfortunate events was apparently not enough to convince her of his waywardness. It was not long before she got a glimpse of his character for herself though. A few months after their wedding, he got engaged to another lady while living with his second wife. She divorced him too and left the country. He got married to a third wife, who would also follow the trend by divorcing him and leaving the country.

Years later, I would coincidentally meet his third wife in Saint Lucia, who told me he was shot dead trying to escape from the police. The story was that he was convicted for a drug-related crime and went to prison. He and another inmate schemed to escape the prison, but their plan was an unsuccessful one. He was shot by the police and died on sight. Despite the traumatic experiences I had faced as a result of this man, hearing of his death was sad. After all, one never truly forgets their first bouts of young love and their first marriage, even if both were formed on a foundation of deceit. I met with his family a while later to give my condolences and offer a few comforting words. Their son was not good to me but the family were always supportive of me, so I owed them that much.

Nursing and Silver Linings

Finally, in October 1981, I began the practical nursing programme, which was a two-year Licenced Practical Nurse (LPN) programme. There were about twelve of us in the LPN group and there were other nurses in the registered nursing programme. It was a great experience for the group to be surrounded with other people of a similar mindset and perseverance. We all had one goal in mind: to be able to help and heal those who couldn't help themselves. Thankfully, we were all successful and graduated in November 1983.

My LPN Experience

I completed some work experience at the out district at Suddie Hospital which is in the Essequibo area of Guyana. My elder sister Doris was living close to Suddie Hospital, so my out-of-town training experience was good as

I had a familiar face around. I also had the privilege to work at the various health centres for a six-week community experience.

I then worked at Georgetown Public Hospital following my LPN graduation.

To counter the hardship of being a new nurse during my time working at Georgetown Hospital, I took part in the yearly nurses' concert as a dancer in the dance group. I am not the best of singers, but I was also a part of the nurses' choir. We called the concert "Nurses in Concert". The name was self-explanatory. Our last Nurses in Concert took place at the National Cultural Centre in Georgetown, Guyana.

Being a part of this last concert was a memory I cherish greatly. The dancing and singing gave me immense joy and a sense of belonging to something wonderful and inspiring. It made me feel good about myself. Now until this day, I still take part in concerts at my place of work with my colleagues during festivities.

My Midwifery Experience

After years of working as a nurse, my desire to become a qualified midwife blossomed. I wanted to help bring babies into this world and support new mothers on their journey. Therefore, I wasted no time in applying to midwifery nursing school in 1986. I was told I had to go out of town again for one year to work along with the midwives to get pre-knowledge experience before going into the midwifery school.

I requested to complete the pre-knowledge training at the hospital in Matthew's Ridge as my family was living there and I grew up there. I also wanted to give back something to the place where I grew up. My request was granted, and I spent a lovely and enlightening year working at Matthew's Ridge hospital. The name of the hospital is Pakera Hospital.

In May 1988, I was granted entrance into the midwifery classroom at Georgetown Hospital after succeeding in the out-of-town training programme. Another dream had come through and the feeling was indescribable. Completing the midwifery programme made me understand more about God's beautiful and creative work that was pregnancy and delivery. It was a great feeling to see the newborn babies open their eyes to a bright brand-new world. The cry of a newborn is incredibly heart-warming. What an awesome God we serve!

I graduated as a midwife in 1990, but it was a year of societal chaos. For one, the Gulf War was in full-fledged action. Nurses were on strike for increased wages and I was amongst them. And because of this wide-spread strike, the hospital was mostly run by the army.

During this period of strike, my sister Jennifer went into labour with my niece Mellissa. Though I had vowed to not go back to the hospital until we received our well-deserved pay, I couldn't leave my sister alone and so I went to the hospital. There was a limited number of staff there, and the ward sister had expressed how grateful she was that I had reached out at the right time to give a helping hand.

One of my favourite memories is delivering my niece, though it was a difficult delivery. She came flat out at birth and did not cry at first. She had quickly become blue in the face as she was not able to cry. I recalled all that I had learnt in midwifery school and applied it. After some massaging, forceful back slaps and suctioning to clear her airway, she began wailing. My niece now jokes I beat and slapped her at birth. It is funny now, of course, but there certainly is a reason why they advise medical professionals not to look after patients who are their relatives. I had become very worried and distressed during this delivery because it was my sister and the baby I was delivering would be my niece, but I quickly remembered

I had to keep a brave face and get the work done to the best of my ability.

Indeed, I was scared but I could not show it.

After midwifery graduation, it was compulsory for each midwife to work at an out-of-town hospital for six months. I choose to go to Bartica Hospital and again my request had been granted. I had the privilege of working there with some amazing doctors, nurses and other amazing staff. I can remember going shopping with my nurse friends Sharon, Charlyn and others on our off days. It was a lovely time and I did enjoy working there.

My stay at this nurses' hostel was only on an on-call basis. The midwife only attended for deliveries, but I do not think I can count the number of deliveries I participated in because there were so many. So many beautiful lives were brought into the world, and I wonder where those babies, now adults, are and who they are!

Dream of a New Life Abroad

I did not serve my full six months at Bartica Hospital as I now had even bigger dreams of going abroad to work as a nurse. I decided to resign and make plans to travel abroad without first securing a job overseas. It was risky but I knew my God was great, and I have always had a knack for the exciting unknown. It was like walking up a staircase in the dark without seeing the next step or fully understanding what sat at the top of the stairs. I guess that is what we call faith in God. I had some relief in knowing that some of my nursing friends had already left Guyana shortly after the strike for more wages, which was unfortunately not granted after the strike. So, I knew I too could handle the adventure.

The only thing was I did not know where my flight passage would come from or where I was going to stay. I did not even choose which country I was going to migrate to, but all I knew was I needed to spread my wings. I brainstormed and came up with a few different countries.

In the end, I decided it would be Saint Lucia as I knew friends and family there. It was a safe, yet exciting option.

I was given a lovely farewell party at Bartica Hospital. I remember a doctor told me I would make it anywhere because I was hard working, and that stuck with me as I travelled through life.

I returned to the city a few days later and told my older sister Doris I was going to Saint Lucia. She asked me if I already had a job waiting for me there.

I replied, "No."

She stared at me incredulously for a second and then said, "Well, okay! If that is what you want, go for it."

Saint Lucia Bound

My sister Doris and her husband paid my first passage out of Guyana to travel to Saint Lucia. My mother and my cousin Yvette paid the $500 for my working transcript. The money I was making as a nurse at the time in Guyana was only for rent and bills. It seemed that many nurses, including myself, were unable to save for even a rainy day.

I left Guyana in April 1991 and landed on Saint Lucia's soil. I believe the Gulf War was ending around that time as well, so times were looking up. The friend who had promised to collect me at the Saint Lucian airport did not show up and had left me deserted in a strange new country. Luckily, I had taken some items from Guyana for some friends in Saint Lucia and they agreed to keep me until I found a place to live. Even now, I feel entirely grateful to the Drakes family who helped me when I had literally nowhere to lay my head. They made my stay comfortable and I was treated well.

I passed the first nursing interview and I was told as soon as they received the working transcript, I could start the job. As it turns out, Saint Lucia was recruiting nurses in abundance, so God sent me there at the right time. However, my transcript was delayed, so I was waiting for three months before I began working.

I was employed at Victoria Hospital in Saint Lucia from 1991 to 1998. I sometimes worked in the medical and surgical unit as well as the emergency unit and operating theatre. But I spent most of my years there working in the paediatric unit, so I had the privilege of dealing with babies and young children after my short stint at Bartica Hospital as a midwife.

I remember working in the paediatric unit on a night shift when Hurricane Debbie swept through the island. The kids were terrified and, to be honest, so was I. We thought that night would never end, but like most things, thanks to God, it did. There were many roadblocks from landslides and fallen trees on my way home. The island had been so badly damaged I did not get home until around midday due to all the diversions after the night duty.

Faith in God Beyond Extreme

Miracle Baby

I got married again in Saint Lucia in 1993 after twelve years divorced from my first husband. After years of working with babies and kids in the paediatric unit, I wanted my own child to look after. But time and time again, I miscarried. I had three miscarriages and was told by the doctor I probably waited too long to have children and I may not be able to carry a baby to full term. I had spent years focusing on my career and becoming the best version of myself, and was now being told this might hinder my chances at becoming a mother. I was heartbroken.

I prayed and trusted God to allow me to carry to full term and asked him to give me a healthy child. Finally, when I was thirty-three years old, I gave birth to my beautiful daughter six days before my birthday. The doctor was wrong. Even the gynaecologist was surprised I did not have another miscarriage. God had answered my prayers. What I learnt from this was that sometimes when the doctor says no, God says yes. Sometimes man says there's no chance, God says just watch this. It was a great blessing when my daughter Crystal entered the world, and she remains a great blessing to me and my family today.

I think back to one day in particular when I was heavily pregnant with Crystal. I was going to pick up the new baby clothes that were washed and hanging on the clothing line on my veranda. I lived in an apartment below another one who also had a veranda above mine. It was a lovely compound. As I opened the door to the veranda, I felt a sudden unbearable thirstiness I could not ignore. Without thought, I closed the veranda door and made to go back to the kitchen for a glass of water. As soon as I closed the door, the veranda from the upstairs house collapsed. Some men were building something upstairs and throwing all the bricks on the roof of the upstairs veranda. I was shaken and stood behind the closed veranda door stunned, thinking that had I not turned back to get a glass of water, my daughter and I would have been crushed. I thanked God profusely for protecting me and my daughter. God was determined that this child should survive...

My mother, my sister Jennifer and her two daughters Lathicia and Mellissa helped me to babysit Crystal. They came from Guyana to live in Saint Lucia before I had my daughter, so it was a blessing to have them there and have a community to help raise my daughter.

As of today, Crystal has completed her English degree at Queen Mary University of London in 2018 and has completed her second degree and master's in law at University of Law in 2021. She is now pursuing a career in law. Glory be to God.

Back to Where Dreams Were Birthed

The birth of my daughter reminded me and reassured me that nothing was impossible with God. In 1997, I bought a house in West Bank, Guyana as I was becoming a little homesick. I thought of going back to Guyana to complete the General Registered Nurses' Programme. After applying the first time, I was not given a place in the nursing school at the public hospital in Guyana as there was no vacancy. Therefore, I decided to contact the private nursing school at St Joseph Mercy Hospital in 1998. I was told that with my qualifications and experience abroad I would be accepted but had to pay a large sum of money for a three-year contract. It would take a lot of money out of my pocket, but I was satisfied knowing it would be a great opportunity to widen my skill set and knowledge. I also knew I'd be free to leave Guyana after the programme to return to Saint Lucia or anywhere else in the world if needs be with a much stronger CV. My husband was not onboard with this idea at first, but eventually agreed with my decision. I resigned from Victoria Hospital in Saint Lucia in early July 1998, and I began another three-year nursing programme in September 1998 at St Joseph Mercy Hospital School of Nursing, Georgetown, Guyana.

My daughter Crystal was just under two years old, but I took her with me. We initially stayed at the house I bought in the countryside, but I was constantly running late to class. There was a large river that ran between the house I lived in and the nursing school, so we had to cross a floating bridge every day. Sometimes the floating bridge was closed off for long hours and I had to cross the river in a speeding boat with my daughter so she could stay with my sister who helped to babysit her when I was working.

It was a strenuous and dangerous journey to have to make often, so I decided to rent my house and used the incoming rent to lease an apartment closer to the nursing school in the city. The apartment was big, so it ended up doubling as a study room as some of the nurses would visit sometimes after classes to revise as a team. With my sister babysitting Crystal, taking her to preschool and me not having to worry about the floating bridge and the frightful speed boat every morning, life was easier.

The three years in the classroom and working in the units, theatre and clinics were hard work but God got me through. The nursing director was a very serious woman and every morning she refused to start the class unless we all prayed and sang along to worship music.

One day, she said to us, "Do not make all the money you paid for this school go to waste. Pass the exams for yourself and your family. Walk out of here proud."

And indeed, we did. In 2001, I completed the three-year Registered Nurse Programme.

But the end of my nursing programme would also be marked by something dire: the Twin Towers attack on 11th September 2001. In one of our last classes, the director called us from the classroom to show us the news. It was horrifying and heartbreaking. We all stood gaping at the television in absolute silence and disbelief. I still cannot fathom the grief the families of those victims are still dealing with today.

Bittersweet

I was eager for the final nursing programme exam results to be published before my birthday on 3rd November. I promised my family in Saint Lucia I was going to come back for my birthday and I also wanted to see my daughter who had gone back to Saint Lucia two months prior.

The results were published on 2nd November. So, that afternoon, I called my sister Jennifer in Saint Lucia to give her the good news. I had passed with flying colours. But on the other side of the phone, she did not welcome my message with joy and I immediately knew something was wrong. The same day my results came out, my mother had high blood pressure, starting the night before, and no one said anything to me as they did not want to make me even more stressed than I was waiting for my exam results. Jennifer said that because my mother's blood pressure had skyrocketed, she suffered a stroke. My celebration ended abruptly.

My big sister organised a flight for me right away and the next morning, I was on a plane to Saint Lucia, on my birthday as I wanted, but without the happiness I had initially anticipated. We landed in Barbados for an hour, which gave me ample time to stress some more in isolation. I reached Saint Lucia at 3 p.m. on my birthday. I asked the taxi driver to drop me at home to drop off my bag, then I went straight to the hospital. I spent the rest of my birthday with my mother at the hospital. The nurses knew me as I had worked there.

Passing my exams was one achievement I did not celebrate as my mother was sick. She never fully recovered from the stroke and she had to use a walking stick everywhere after. Ten years later, she got sick with cancer, and she was given eighteen months to live. I visited Saint Lucia when my mother was supposed to be having surgery for the cancer. But that same day, the surgery was cancelled because Saint Lucia was expecting a terrible hurricane. The hospital staff asked everyone to take their families home. Only the extremely ill patients were kept in the hospital. I took my mother home one hour before the hurricane began full-fledged. The torrential rain, the beating wind, thunder and lightning lasted from 2 p.m. and carried on through the late hours of the evening.

We were all scared for numerous reasons but my mother kept saying to us, "Stay calm, the hurricane will be over."

It is funny that she was the one in pain, yet she was also the one comforting the rest of us. I guess a mother never stops being a mother. She was always a person with a strong faith in God and in turn she has built my faith with so many things.

The hurricane caused absolute havoc to the island. My daughter and I had to go to the international airport by buying a plane ticket to fly across the island from the capital city. The main roads were damaged by the strong winds and so we could not drive to the airport. I felt sad and desolate leaving my mother in the condition she was in, whilst I travelled home.

She lived two years after the cancer diagnosis instead of the eighteen months the doctor had predicted. She had complained of pain in her side, but the doctor told her it was muscle pain without fully investigating the issue. Unfortunately, the mere "muscle pain" turned out to be cancer, which was eventually diagnosed a while afterwards. She battled with cancer for two years, but her suffering is over now. She died on 12th March 2012. I had the privilege of seeing her and caring for her a few days before she passed. I saw her take her last breath. She died in her home in Guyana. She requested to be cared for in Guyana where she was born and grew up, and she was given the privilege by God to die peacefully amongst her family and children.

When I returned to Saint Lucia in November 2001, I was accepted for a job at Tapion Hospital which is a private hospital. I was given the job by Sister John who is a wonderful and supportive sister; under her management, I strived. To be registered in Saint Lucia as a full registered nurse and midwife, I had to take the Saint Lucia bar exams, which I was successful at. I returned briefly to St.

Joseph Mercy Hospital in 2002 in Guyana for my graduation. It was lovely to catch up with everyone else from the batch after being away for a year. But all of this success could not take away the fact that my mother's health had deteriorated. I was grateful to God that my mother, along with my sister Doris and my daughter Crystal, made it to my nursing graduation.

An American Getaway

My family and I went for a trip to New York City in September 2004 for two weeks. We stopped by one of my aunts in Brooklyn who is sadly no longer with us.

I had dreams from a young age to travel to America. We had always heard about this faraway country that was amazing, with its superstar celebrities, fancy jobs and amazing food. But the reality was different. During the nights we were there, we heard so many bottles being broken around the streets and countless gunshots. It was terrifying, to say the least. One day, my aunt, my daughter and I were going to the supermarket and had to run for cover at the side of a car after gunshots started going off. Two young boys were shooting at each other in the bright daylight.

On the positive side, some parts of New York City are beautiful, and we had the chance to catch up with some friends. I got the opportunity to live with a young married couple and teach them how to care for their newborn baby. They improved on the care and were grateful for my short help.

Yet, I was extremely happy when we returned to Saint Lucia in one piece.

The broken bottles and the gunshots scared me. As far as I was aware, my dream to go to America was satisfied, but I now had no intentions of living there for a long period of time ever.

New Pastures

In 2005, one of my friends, who also happened to be a nurse that migrated from Guyana to Saint Lucia, gave me a phone number. She told me it was a number for an agency located in England and they were recruiting for nurses from the Caribbean. She was the type to make jokes we all find hilarious, so naturally I laughed, thinking this was another one of her stories. But she told me to call and seemed very serious about it.

After some deliberation and doubt as to if working in England was something that could ever be a possibility, I called the phone number. It rang and rang and before I knew it, there was a voice on the other end of the line. The number was real.

They wasted no time in setting my telephone interview for the next day. The interview was a success and just a mere one week later, my working documents were in my hand. Another eight days and my daughter and I were on a flight to Barbados' embassy to collect our legal papers. Two weeks after that, Crystal and I were on the biggest jet I'd ever been on to London, England. This was in March 2005.

It happened all so quickly I do not think I ever really stopped to understand the amazingness of it all. My ambition and faith had taken me miles and miles away from home. We spent one week at my aunt Patsy's flat in Deptford, London, getting used to wearing coats every time we stepped out the door, and taking in a culture significantly different from the vibrant Caribbean.

Life in the UK

I started my first job as a registered nurse in England in a care home called Churchview Care Home in the small and beautiful town of Swindon. One week after arriving in England, the company sent a taxi to take us to Swindon. It was about an hour's drive outside of the capital. The further we travelled from London, the more greenery we saw. As we peered out the taxi's window, we saw farms dotted with cows, horses, sheep and empty plots of land as far as the eyes could see. The ruralness of it all was reminiscent of home in Matthew's Ridge, but soon enough we entered Swindon and the brick houses and small shops came into view.

My husband soon followed and came to England six weeks after we arrived. He had stayed back in Saint Lucia a while longer to tie up loose ends. My husband being in England provided some ease as we were able to share childcare of Crystal who was only seven years old at the time. Luckily, the care home I worked at offered my husband a job very quickly and we were able to settle in to our new lives relatively easily.

During my three years working at Churchview Care Home, I had the privilege of working at one of the company's care homes in Cardiff, Wales. The home was short of staff, and I was asked to go and help the situation for two months. I was happy to meet some of the nurses I knew from Guyana working there. Whilst there, I had the opportunity to complete training in Food Hygiene as well as Moving and Handling, which enabled me to be the trainer for Churchview Care Home when I eventually went back. I returned to Cardiff for several training courses. Cardiff is a beautiful city and, in fact, Wales as a whole has some beautiful landscapes and places to visit.

The manager for the Churchview Care Home treated us like family and soon she became like our second family in a city where we barely knew anyone. Despite her classy and pristine appearance and high position, she was humble and down to earth. Although she had no obligations to, she gave us a tour of Swindon and made sure we were well settled in and always looked out for us. I still claim to this day that she is one of the kindest people I have ever met. She was from Barbados and she has since returned to Barbados following her retirement.

During our time in Swindon, it was not very multicultural and it wasn't uncommon to be the only black family sitting in a restaurant or shopping in the popular centre. It was something we never really spoke about, but it was noticeable. Thankfully, I cannot recall encountering any overt racial issues.

Crystal started primary school shortly after we got to Swindon. She was the only black child in her grade and probably in the school. It worried me at first that she might be excluded or treated unfairly, but thankfully the teachers were all kind and treated her like every other pupil. I remember she took part in one of the school's concerts depicting the biblical story of Joseph and the multicoloured coat. Despite being the only dark-skinned child in the group, she fitted right in and she looked very pleased standing up there on the stage. It was a beautiful concert and I would never forget it.

My family and I had enjoyed living in the small town of Swindon, but eventually I started to dream of living in the big lustrous city of London. What I did not know was that those dreams would become reality sooner rather than later.

En Route to London

When my daughter was only ten years old, she saw an advert on the TV regarding an acting, modelling, dancing and commercial school in Piccadilly, London. She always took part in concerts at day care, preschool and junior school, so she was always interested in the arts. Within seconds, Crystal had taken the telephone number down for the TV advert and called the acting school without my husband's or my knowledge. The person she spoke to asked her to put one of her parents or guardians on the phone. I first thought she was joking or playing a prank on us but sure enough, there was someone on the line.

I took the call and the person explained who they were and what they did. It was an acting school in Piccadilly Circus that had launched the creative careers of many child actors and actresses. We were given dates for the acting audition in London. The auditions were at Haye Market Street in Piccadilly, London in 2008.

I remember the audition was a Saturday afternoon and finished in the late evening. We were given the outcome of the audition that same evening and Crystal was selected to start attending the school from September 2008. It was an evening of thanksgiving to God. Crystal began her two-year programme in the acting school.

It was like a miracle that happened so quickly. One impromptu and random phone call made by Crystal in August 2008 landed us in London in September 2008.

The programme was £3,000 but it was worth it.

My request to be transferred to another care home by the same company in London was granted immediately after I showed the manager the acting school's acceptance contract. This was the way God used my daughter to grant our prayers to move us from Swindon to London.

We love Swindon and miss the friends we made there, but to be quite honest, I do prefer living in London as it is more diverse and multicultural and there are many more things to do in your free time.

We were also happy to move to London to be closer to my aunt Patsy, who was still living in Deptford, and so we were able to visit her more often. I guess it was the will of God to be closer to her as her health was deteriorating and we were able to assist her husband with whatever help we could provide. She was in and out of hospital a lot due to her ill health. Sadly, she passed away in December 2013. She had always wanted me to come to England and work as a nurse, so I'm glad she lived long enough to see her wish come through.

My Daughter's Academic Years

My daughter was accepted into a secondary school in October 2008, so she would be the new girl once again amongst her year group but she would go on to have an amazing five years there. We lived within walking distance from the school, so it was as if everything was falling into place perfectly. Crystal completed her secondary school education in 2013, then completed her college education in 2015.

Crystal completed college with the excellent grades required to get her into her first-choice university, which was Queen Mary University of London. She studied and finished her three-year English degree with honours in July 2018. Her graduation was awesome; her father and I couldn't keep the smiles off of our faces. Glory be to God. I am so proud of her.

In December 2019, Crystal decided she would like to do a law master's degree. She had been thinking about it for a while, but needed some encouragement due to feeling it was too late for her to go back to university. It had been a year since she had graduated from her undergraduate degree and like many young adults fresh out of university, career jobs were hard to come by. I explained to her that whether she did the law master's or not, time would pass regardless, so why not go for it. Plus, she was only twenty-three, so she had plenty of time ahead of her still. She immediately wrote her university proposal, and applied to the University of Law in December 2019 and was accepted to start only a month later in January 2020. The same year the COVID-19 pandemic would hit.

Indeed, it was a year of severe unprecedented times, but triumphantly, Crystal was able to complete her studies with the help of technology and made it through the storms. Despite the stress and anxiety that spread across the world, she persevered and was successful in completing her legal master's degree. Soon after completing her studies, she landed a role at a law firm which gave her the experience to launch her legal career.

The child I was so fearful I'd lose in pregnancy was now thriving in life. Nothing is impossible for those who believe and trust in God; just have a little bit of faith.

A Serial Acting Manager

I was stationed on the dementia unit at the first care home I worked for in London. I assisted with the training for Food Hygiene and Moving and Handling due to the experience I had gained previously. My employment contract at this home was only thirty-seven hours, and because London is an expensive city to live, I needed more money to keep up with the rent, bills and food. I applied for a second job and was able to secure another role quickly for one day a week for a higher rate of pay. I was only allowed to complete one day at another workplace due to work permit restrictions.

It was during this time I witnessed a carer abusing an elderly resident, and I promptly reported this to the manager. The carer was not suspended, despite another carer witnessing the abuse as well, because she denied the act. As a trainer of safeguarding, I took my role very seriously and therefore knew I had to escalate the matter if it wasn't being taken seriously from within the home.

The manager had refused to action any consequences and I reported the case to the head office who ensured they would investigate the matter.

I eventually received an apology from both the manager and the head office. But my integrity would not allow me to stay and work under a manager who did not take abuse seriously in the first instance, so I resigned. The manager would eventually resign due to the same incident.

I landed a full-time position in another care home as I had received my resident permit by then and the pay at the new job was better. The manager at this new home taught me a great deal about managerial work. She treated her staff, residents and visitors with kindness and respect. But in April 2010, that manager resigned. The only nurse in the building who knew about managerial work was me. The director promoted me to acting manager the day after the manager resigned. There were already plans of the home closing down and being sold, but nothing was yet confirmed and so I accepted the sudden promotion.

I remember greeting a lady at the street corner one morning as she was closing her car door. She responded with a lovely greeting. At that time, I did not know who she was. Later that morning, I was returning to my office after checking the nursing units. I looked over and saw the same lady waiting in the reception area. That was when one of the carers told me I had a visitor waiting to see and speak to me and pointed towards the woman.

I began to laugh and she began to laugh.

She said, "I only just saw you on the street a while ago!" She then introduced herself as a CQC inspector, and she was there to inspect the care home.

It was moments like this that reminded me how important it is to be kind to strangers on the street; you never know who they are or how they may impact your life. A simple greeting could put you on the right side of history. Thankfully, the care home inspection went well. The home passed the inspection with only one minor action plan.

Yet, it would take me years to finally secure a full manager position, and I had long come to suspect my ethnicity had a lot to do with this. There were several occasions where I worked at care homes as deputy nurse manager, being exposed to the office job and what it took to lead an entire home, but when the different managers resigned, I was never given the opportunity of being promoted. On three different occasions, I was promoted to acting manager for months on end. When it was time to hire an actual manager, I completed excellent interviews and was told I managed the home well as acting manager. But each and every time, the outcome would be a white person who would show up claiming to be the new manager.

Other times I had interviews for the manager positions and was told I was successful at the initial interview. When I was asked to go for the second part of the interview, usually to meet a higher up who was most likely a white person, I would smash the interview, but would never hear from them again. I could not understand why I was told I passed the interviews and they were excellent, then be completely dismissed.

I was acting manager for five months at a previous care home. The home passed an important inspection under my management, yet when it was time to put a manager in position, I was told that both of us did an excellent job at the interview, but the other interviewee had three years' extra experience. So, I was very surprised when I then had to teach the new manager everything about the care home and about managing a home. I finally concluded I had been taken advantage of and could not work with someone who I had to teach continuously, when I was not accepted for the manager post. And so, I left, disappointed, but proud of my decision.

A SERIAL ACTING MANAGER

I spent a short time at another care home as I was recruited as a deputy manager, and I was not told the dementia unit did not have a manager. I was asked to manage the unit doing a manager's job but still getting a deputy manager's pay with the promise of eventually being given the manager position. When I realised no manager was ever going to come and I was once again being used as an acting manager whilst getting a deputy's pay, I knew I had to leave yet another job. It was very frustrating to be treated in such a manner. This all happened to me around 2012 when my mother was very sick. My mother passed away in March 2012, which was an added stress. It was not healthy and I was not going to let anyone treat me with disrespect, so I left the job after I returned from my mother's funeral.

I took another job, where I spent six months, as I was not told at the interview that the home was closing down soon. I decided to take a deputy manager job there as it was a three-minute walk from where I was living. To have the qualifications for a job, the knowledge, being successful at the interviews and still being disrespected can be truly soul-crushing and play with your self-esteem.

A Different Path

In January 2013, I felt it was time to take a break from nursing and working in a care home. I contemplated between returning to Guyana or applying for another job. Childcare came to mind, and because I've always been very nurturing, I thought it would be a fitting career to experience. I applied to do the Childcare Homebase course at Wandsworth Early Years Childcare Providers training centre. This commenced in February 2013 and completed in March 2013 as it was only a six-week training course. I registered with Ofsted and started full-time childcare for one year. But some parents were not paying the childcare fees effectively and this went on for some time. Despite my love for childcare and running my own business, I went back to nurse management as the lack of payment from parents was starting to result in low funds. It was no longer enough to pay my rent, bills, food and necessities.

I went back to the care home in late 2014. I got a job in the north of England, but only spent a short while there due to the distance, train delays and cancellations from London. I asked the same agency that had got me this job to look for a job closer to where I was living. The long travelling was getting exhausting. Some afternoons it would take me three hours to get home by bus due to busy traffic and steady transport cancellations. It was especially worse during the winter, having to wait long hours for the train. The agency finally got me a very good position in June 2015 closer to where I was living in London, and I am still with that company presently.

I began working as a deputy nurse manager in June 2015 and once again I became acting manager in October 2015. I finally caught my break and was promoted to the care home manager on 3rd November 2016 due to hard work and dedication. It was on my birthday that I received the promotion and so that made it more special. I was registered as the care home manager in December 2016. I thoroughly enjoy working for the company and I love my job. And I can say I am treated with kindness and respect. It is by far the best care home company I have worked for, and I am happy to be able to maintain and run the care home in a person-centred approach. My loudest thanks has to be given to the boss and directors of Sovereign company, my staff, the residents and the visitors as they all make my place of work a happier one. Glory be to God.

Deserved Breaks and the Fruits of My Labour

Paris 2018

My daughter and I visited Paris for three days in May 2018. We did everything one does in Paris: taking photos in front of the Eiffel Tower, eating food we could not pronounce on a moving boat and enjoying being tourists. It was a lovely but short time.

On our way to the Paris airport, the taxi driver told us they were going to have a celebration the next day in the capital. He said it would be nice for us to go and enjoy the culture and gatherings. He was from the Caribbean but had lived in Paris for a few years, and was very excited about the upcoming event. We told him that had we known about it earlier, we may have booked to stay a bit longer, but we were unable to as we were travelling back to London that same day. He was quite friendly and chatted most of the way to the airport, telling us about Paris like a tour guide.

The following day, we travelled back to London. While we were waiting to board the flight back home, we noted there were many soldiers at the airport but thought nothing of it. When we got back to London that afternoon, the evening news mentioned there had been an attack near the aforementioned celebration that took a life and left many others injured. That had been the same event the taxi driver was telling us about, but none of us knew that it would end in tragedy.

Reunions Galore

Later that year and in 2019, I decided another big break was needed. And so, I planned and organised a family and friends reunion in both Saint Lucia and Guyana. I had been overseas for a few years and it was a wonderful feeling to finally hug, talk, meet and eat with my family and friends that I hadn't seen in a while. In hindsight, I am glad I did this because no one knew that only a year later, many people would not be able to see each other at all due to the COVID-19 pandemic and lockdown. It makes the memory of spending time together with loved ones that much more precious.

In 2018, I held the reunion at one of Guyana's popular restaurants with food and flavours that were reminiscent of my childhood. The evening was spectacular. Saint Lucia's reunion with family was also beautiful, and was held in two different restaurants with the warm tropical ocean breeze blowing slightly in the background. A far difference to the greyness and coldness of London.

But in 2019, we decided to hold the reunion a little closer to home and so it was held at my big sister Doris' home in Guyana. Doris is the founder of the Children's Sparkle Group by which she takes care of various underprivileged children in a Guyanese community called Sophia. There are some faithful donors like myself and others who ensure the children's needs are being met. God is the greatest helper for this group. My mother used to love helping children in need, and she asked us to continue to do the same after she was gone. So, for the reunion, it made sense for Doris to organise a lovely concert with the children and then we would serve lunch to the community at the same time. It was a lovely way to get family and friends together and the kids got to enjoy a fun day out.

I also used our 2019 trip to Guyana to introduce Crystal to Matthew's Ridge and Port Kaituma and show her the little towns that I grew up in. I showed Crystal the school I attended and we travelled through the area of the Jim Jones temple. This brought back strong sad memories of that murderous day many decades ago.

Alabama 2019

In February 2019, in the spirit of travelling some more, I decided to revisit America, despite my not so pleasant previous experience in New York. This time around, I visited an old-time friend, Juliet Graham-Thornhill, in Huntsville, Alabama. It was the first time I was seeing her after thirty-five years, since she had opened up her home to me to stay before my nursing career took off. She had left for America years back, and when she finally did visit Guyana again, I had already migrated to Saint Lucia and so we had narrowly missed each other.

Her home and family were welcoming and warm, and I was instantly made to feel comfortable despite not having seen each other in a while. She also took me to her church and the service that day was wonderful. I was later received with a big welcome banquet, filled with different types of food. Juliet had told me I would meet up with one or two people I knew from back home, but instead, I saw about five different people I had known from Guyana. The feeling of being around those who had known me when I was just a teenage or in my twenties, and now seeing everyone well into adulthood, was exhilarating.

Juliet drove me through the streets of Alabama. From what I saw, Alabama was a beautiful place and very peaceful. But as she drove by, she pointed to some areas that were once cotton fields used during the days of slavery. It was surreal to look upon the area that people who looked like me once slaved away under terrible conditions and against their will at the hands of other brutal human beings. I felt an immense sadness as Juliet spoke of the history of slavery and the things our ancestors were forced to do.

I was only in America for a week, but I wanted to make the most of my time there, so Juliet and I took the opportunity to fly over to New York City, making a quick stop off in North Carolina to visit other family and friends. But on our way to New York, it was a stormy evening and the plane was unable to land in New York as the winds were pushing the plane here and there every time the pilot attempted to land the plane. The flight was very rough most of the way from North Carolina to New York, to say the least. There was a moment when the plane was descending to land. The winds pushed it off course and it was plunging down towards the river. I really thought that was it for us at that moment. But at the last minute, the pilot gave a steep dive upwards away from the danger. I was terrified, but we could not do anything else but pray. It reminded me of the last experience I had those many years ago when I was travelling with my sister and the wheels of the plane had refused to come down. Like that last time, this plane too had to circle around the airport multiple times before we were able to land.

"Thank God for a safe landing," I had whispered.

When we reached New York safely, we planned to connect with various friends like Heppie, Wendy, my cousin Shevon, Gail and a few others, but time was limited and I only had two days left in New York. My ticket to America was only booked for one week, so I had to return to Huntsville after the two days in New York before travelling back to London. Nevertheless, we had a wonderful day out in downtown Brooklyn and this short trip was definitely needed. I almost forgot that this was the place of broken bottles and gunshots!

The following day, we travelled to Nashville to meet Juliet's family because it was Valentine's Day. We all had dinner at the Cheesecake Factory restaurant. It was a great dining experience. The following day, full and buzzing with new memories, I travelled back to London. America was not all bad after all.

Scotland 2019

Later that year, I travelled to another city I had never seen before which was Aberdeen, Scotland. The flight from London to Scotland was only one hour which was convenient. In May 2019, my daughter and I visited two friends there. My friend Sherri invited us for her birthday party. It was a lovely celebration and it was nice to meet up with friends and chat about old times. I guess this year was one for reconnecting with my past.

My friend Genevieve showed us a little around Aberdeen. It was a much quieter place than I had envisioned and very green, filled with fresh air. We did not get to explore much as we only went for the two-day celebration, but I would definitely like to go back again.

Birthday Celebration November 2019

Some of my friends visited me in London for my birthday on 3rd November 2019. Juliet visited from Huntsville, Alabama, so I was lucky to see her twice in one year after thirty-five years apart. My friends from Bristol, England, Roxanne, Sahai and Abigale, also visited. Jessica from St Kitts and Nevis who was at Roehampton University at the time and other friends and staff from work all gathered with us for a lovely evening. I felt blessed to have shared my birthday with wonderful friends who travelled from all over to celebrate with me. And although they were visitors in my house, that was the first birthday party I did not have to do any decorating or cooking. Everything was done for me. I am truly blessed.

Swift Changes

COVID-19 Pandemic

In 2020, almost out of nowhere, we were hit with the COVID-19 pandemic. It was a difficult time for most people and we were truly living through unprecedented times, but I held the belief that God was good and he would get us out of the chaos.

My personal struggle was ensuring my residents in the care home were not made vulnerable to this killer disease. But just like many other care homes, sadly we lost a small number of residents. Thankfully, with the correct implementations, actions and infection prevention training, we were able to clear the home quickly of COVID-19 and it has been like this for months now. We adhered to and followed the government guidelines strictly to prevent the spread of the virus in the care home. With the support of the care home's directors, the district nurses, the doctors and the staff, we were able to manage and keep things under control. But alongside this, I also utilised daily prayers.

There were often times when my staff were off sick with the virus and many were nurses. As a nurse by profession, I was able to go back to my nursing roots and help out in the units. I felt I was doing my small part in a much bigger picture. It was very scary constantly hearing the news every day about the virus and being exposed to so many residents and staff, but the work had to be done and I knew God was with me. After all, someone had to care for the residents and patients. I am so thankful to my staff who were very supportive. They went to work despite what was happening in the world and got the job done. I now manage a care home that is a hundred percent vaccinated against COVID-19.

In February 2021, I contracted COVID-19 but, thank God, I recovered quickly within eight days, but I isolated for fourteen days. My daughter, who lived in the same house as me, did not contract the virus because we followed the infection control guidelines.

Post-Pandemic Freedom

After months of lockdown and stringent rules, the prospect of travel seemed far-fetched. We had cancelled our flight to Barcelona in 2020 and hadn't thought of travelling until everything had calmed down.

In 2021, my daughter and I were fully vaccinated but travel, tiers and isolation periods were still very unpredictable. Finally, in 2022, my stepson got engaged and invited us to his wedding in Guyana, and this was not something we wanted to miss and so we took our chances. After almost three years, we purchased our flights to the Caribbean. Except this time, it was different to our 2019 trip; we had to wear a mask throughout our nine-hour flight and were made to wear a hand band proving our vaccination status once we landed in Saint Lucia and Guyana. Three years prior, this may have seemed like a scene out of a dystopian film. Nevertheless, we were finally reunited with family and friends once again and everything felt somewhat back to normal.

The vacation was amazing and we took the opportunity to enjoy ourselves in the best way possible. We stayed at the beautiful family hotel Bay Gardens Resort, which had the sand and ocean right outside our doorstep. They played reggae and calypso and all the music that makes the Caribbean as vibrant as it is. My niece hosted us in her new spacious home and cooked us a great feast for our family reunion. We sang karaoke into the late night and ate food until it was impossible to chew anymore. We then travelled across to Guyana in June 2022 where we stopped at Guyana's Princess Hotel. If I was to tell my younger self that I would be staying at a luxurious hotel in Guyana for a week straight, I might've laughed from disbelief. But here I was, surrounded by family, love and gratitude.

Our trip back to London on 4th July 2022 was a long one as the check-in process at Saint Lucia's airport was four hours, followed by an hour of delay on the runway due to dangerous thunderstorms and lightning. The nine-hour flight back to London was a scary one due to constant and heavy turbulence and the funny noises of the plane engine. Once we touched down at London Gatwick, I released a breath I did not know I was holding for nine hours straight. But I was joyful and grateful to have seen my family after the pandemic chaos.

A New Era

Looking back now, and writing this, has made it clear to me how far I have come. From a young girl with little money but big dreams, to a grown woman with a child and a successful career. I can only praise God. Now, as I enter my sixties, I feel a shift in the atmosphere. I can only imagine the great things that lie in front of me and I am excited about it.

And indeed, we have all entered a new era. The passing of Queen Elizabeth has marked that somewhat. There are feelings of sadness for her passing, yet feelings of happiness for the new king. There is a mixture of feelings. Even for those who never really understood the monarchy, the queen was always there as a sign of stability, tradition and comfort. Although, this change is something the United Kingdom will gradually get used to. After seventy years of a queen being the head of state, we now have a king. It is weird to say. But, may God bless the king with good health and a long reign, and may he continue to bless us all.

Thanks

Thanks to God Almighty, friends and families and strangers along the way.

Thanks to Almighty God for everyone and everything and for giving me the inspiration to write this book.

Thanks to my daughter Crystal Johnson for her support, motivation and cooperation.

Thanks to my directors and staff for their support and cooperation in motivating me to write this book.

Thanks to all my family, friends and church family. Thanks to my neighbours.

Some people crossed our path for the better. Some were for a blessing, and some were for a lesson. I will share some of the people who crossed my path for a blessing.

My entire family are in my life as a blessing from God. Thanks to all my family for your love. My friends, neighbours and strangers are there for a blessing in some way or another. Thanks for your love.

One of my mum's cousins by the name of Jean Rogers is a lady who is kind, humble and likes to share. We call her Cousin Jean. I remember as a child my family wasn't rich, and Cousin Jean wasn't rich. Just like my mum, we never left Cousin Jean's house without her packing a bag with some little goodies. Cousin Jean's attitude towards giving has made me think about how someone could have little and still give. My mum taught us the same about giving: don't mind how little we have. I am not surprised when my family and I have the giving and sharing attitude. I am thankful to God for blessing Cousin Jean in an amazing way. She lives in England now too. What an amazing woman.

Leslyn and Heppilena Brazilo and family kept me in their home when I was getting settled in the city in Guyana. Leslyn was like a mother to me. She used to make sure everything was okay in the house. Amazing family. A family who loves the Lord.

I can remember Pinkie and Heppie used to invite me to the Seventh Day Adventist church. They motivated me in serving the Lord. Pinkie kept me at her apartment in Georgetown and fed me when I was waiting to start my nursing job in the city. Another example of kindness.

My sister Doris and her husband gave me my first plane passage out of Guyana to Saint Lucia as in those days plane tickets were expensive and still are. Doris wasn't worried about if she would get her money back or not. She is a woman who trusts God for doing wonders, which he did.

Sydney Drakes, Lennox Drakes and family: I am very grateful to them. They played a great part in supporting me until I officially started my job in Saint Lucia.

Gem, my cousin Lorraine Wilkinson and my cousin Gale Assanah, who is no longer with us, were people who granted me emotional support as we lived in Saint Lucia together. Amazing people.

The nurses, doctors and other staff from Victoria Hospital and Tapion Hospital are amazing people. Sister John gave me my job at Tapion Hospital. She is a kind and lovely lady.

Nurse Rita Ramdayal was the director for nursing at St Joseph Mercy Hospital. Amazing lady. She taught me and the other nurses that there were no classes without morning worship to God. We put God first and he has blessed us all well.

My sister Jenny and her daughters Tisha and Mellissa in Saint Lucia. They are amazing people. They were so helpful to me when my daughter was a baby. I used to say to Tisha, "Don't touch my stove." When I go to the supermarket and return Tisha finished cooking and wash. Mellissa was only five and wanted to play mother. Bless them.

My mum too was an amazing lady who used to babysit my daughter for me. Also thanks to my sister Doris who used to babysit Crystal when I was at the nursing school at St Joseph Mercy Hospital.

My cousin Yvette Wilkinson and my mum paid my transcript money to work in Saint Lucia which was $500 at that time. My cousin Yvette is kind and loving. She didn't even wonder if she would ever be repaid, but she was.

When I was in nursing school at St Joseph Mercy Hospital, my husband Walter Johnson sent financial support every month for three years without fail. My sister Jenny paid half of the nursing contract money which I repaid. Kind and wonderful people.

My friend Gail who gave me the phone number to get the nursing job in England. Gail welcomed my daughter and I in her home in England for a visit. She is an excellent nurse. I worked with her at Tapion Hospital.

Maureen, one of my manager friends, gave my daughter and I a tour of Swindon and London when we first came to England. She welcomed us into her home like family. She returned to Barbados, and we hold her like family now…

Thanks to my manager friend Patience who taught me a lot about the manager job in England in 2009. A kind and humble woman of God.

To all those friends and family who met with us for the family reunion dinner in 2018 and 2019, thank you. It was worthwhile because during the pandemic, people were unable to travel freely. Nevertheless, God's grace and mercies are enough.

To my director and my boss, thanks for giving me the job in your amazing company. I have been working for seven years now in your company and still enjoy my work. To my amazing staff, thank you and keep up the good work.

To my friends Sahai, Roxanne and Abigale, thank you for inviting us to your home for your birthday party. And thank you for coming to my birthday party in 2019 and for helping with the shopping and cooking. Amazing friends. I can remember Sahai went to the teller with her trolley.

I said, "Sahai, put the things together with my things." They were my birthday groceries by the way.

She said, "No, Lynette. I will pay. It's your birthday."

I still remember the baked chicken from Abigale and the vegetable fried rice from Roxanne.

My friend Pinkie travelled all the way from Alabama for my birthday in 2019. Pinkie invited me to her home in Huntsville in 2019 and gave me a tour of Huntsville, Alabama. I received the most amazing welcome party. I met people who I knew from Guyana. She only told me I would see one person but surprised me as I saw five I knew.

Sherri, one of my nurse friends, invited us to her birthday party in Scotland in 2019. I am grateful.

Genevieve Hume, one of my nurse friends, gave me a tour of Scotland. One of the best female drivers I have known.

My elderly church friend Sister Alda is always kind and likes to bake a cake or bring a plant for us. Amazing woman of God that taught me so much about faith in God.

My nephew Josh taught me in his attitude how being humble is. He gave me a tour of St. Thomas, US Virgin Islands. I received some of the most amazing paintings from him. He loves to help people like I do.

Glory be to God. What an awesome God we serve. Gratitude is powerful. I must thank God for life, each new day. Thanks to Almighty God for everything and everyone. Thank God for his grace and mercies and for bringing us this far.

THANKS

Thanks to families and friends, neighbours and strangers along the way. Thanks to my daughter Crystal who played a great role in helping me with the editing of this book.

Thanks to the publishers who are also a great part of this book's success.

I am walking with God and I will continue to walk with God until the day I die. There must be a better world out there for everyone. Only God can take us there.

I end my book by saying all glory be to God the creator of Heaven and Earth. The Almighty God. Thank God for the privilege of allowing me to write this book.

May God bless us all as we continue to strive for a better world.

Reasons for Writing This Book

1. To motivate everyone not to give up on their dreams.
2. To remind everyone that rain does not fall forever and storm clouds always pass over.
3. To remind you that God is a silent helper in trouble.
4. To make sure you believe in yourself and trust in God.

Summary

My story began in the dark looking out towards the light. This is what hope is. Despite the stormy years, by the grace of God, I made it out.

When I was a child, I used to run up and down hills. Sometimes I used to be very exhausted. I can remember looking up to the mountains that seemed so hard to climb. God can still turn things around. I used to look up to the mountains and pray to Almighty God to get me to the top of the mountain.

Dreams sometimes seem hard to come true, but now I have reached the top of the mountain, I believe fully that dreams are possible to all those who believe and trust in God.

There were happy times and there were unhappy times, but my faith and trust in God got me through those stormy times.

My family and I went through difficult days, but we were happy and content with what life had to offer us. My stories will help people to remain strong in faith in good times and bad times.

The stories I have written in my book will encourage people to remain calm and keep looking out at the light when they are in the dark.

My stories also have a lot of testing times that called for a lot of faith and only trusting in God and praying can take us through the trying times.

Glory be to God.

www.ingramcontent.com/pod-product-compliance
Lightning Source LLC
Chambersburg PA
CBHW030042100526
44590CB00011B/295